PARIS

teNeues

CAFE BAR BRASSERIE
le bouledogue
PETITS DEJEUNERS • BREAKFAST
JMB PARIS

PARIS

Photographs by Heiko Lanio
Text by Soraya Elyes Ferchichi

teNeues

ISABELLE ADJANI
SAMI FREY
SAMY NACERI
la repentie
un film de
LAETITIA MASSON
LE 17 AVRIL

Monumentale et intime, Paris est un mythe autant qu'une ville. Elle fait partie de ces cités qui, comme Rome, Jérusalem ou New York, développent une identité singulière, véritablement distincte du pays qui les entoure. Il s'agit bien là d'un art de vivre, qui frappe tout d'abord le regard : Paris, ingénieuse, multiple, secrète et paradoxale met immédiatement en scène ceux qui la traversent, habitants pressés de la capitale ou promeneurs charmés. Ce sont parfois les mêmes, à d'autres moments du jour et de la nuit, car tout invite à y flâner.

« Il est des lieux stériles et des lieux bénis » me confiait l'écrivain Lawrence Durrell lorsqu'il évoquait Paris. « La ville recèle un climat tonifiant, vivifiant, magnétique. Et les gens guettent Paris pour cette raison, sans souvent être conscient que c'est cette énergie qu'ils recherchent. Nous étions toujours informés, nous nous sentions vraiment au centre des choses, même en ne faisant rien, en restant simplement à la terrasse des cafés ».

Cette ville si vaste par son histoire et sa culture, depuis que la tribu gauloise des « Parisii » lui légua son nom, se traverse à pied en un peu plus de deux heures, du Nord au Sud ou d'Ouest en Est. Mais la plus belle avenue de Paris reste la Seine, que jalonnent trente-sept ponts. Car « Fille de la Seine et du Roi », c'est sur ses îlots, puis autour du grand fleuve si propice aux échanges et au commerce, que s'est déployée la ville, jusqu'à choisir son orgueilleuse et légère devise « Fluctuat nec mergitur » : Il flotte sans être submergé.

Longeant ou rejoignant la Seine, les perspectives grandioses de la ville… Ainsi domine, du haut de sa colline, le Palais de Chaillot qui embrasse les jets d'eau des jardins du Trocadéro jusqu'au Pont d'Iéna derrière lequel se dresse la Tour Eiffel dans son écrin verdoyant du Champs de Mars que bordent les Invalides.

Mais l'on peut en quelques rues échapper à ce bel ordonnancement classique, pousser une porte cochère qui s'ouvrira sur un jardin sauvage, découvrir ensuite un petit bar à vins servant des fromages fermiers, franchir l'entrée d'un des cent cinquante musées parisiens, celle d'un carré d'antiquaires où l'on pourra choisir, comme dans l'une des enseignes de la haute couture parisienne, d'admirer tant de créativité ou de se ruiner pour elle.

« Ce n'est pas une ville, c'est un monde » s'émerveillait-on de Paris à l'époque de la Renaissance. C'est peut-être depuis une ville qui fait sans cesse renaître un monde.

Soraya Elyes Ferchichi

Paris, a sprawling giant and yet a very intimate city, is a legend and at the same time a metropolis. Like Rome, Jerusalem, or New York, it is one of those cities that develop a unique identity which completely sets it apart from the rest of the country. And that is probably the result of a way, or better: an art of living that attracts attention before anything else. Paris—creative and multifaceted, concealing and contradictory—is an open stage setting for all who move about within its limits, be they hurried natives or enchanted visitors. Sometimes the same people appear on this stage, just at another time of day or night, for everything in Paris is an invitation to stroll around.

“Paris comprises uncreative and, at the same time, blessed places”, as the author Lawrence Durell confided to me. “The city has an enlivening, fascinating, and magnetizing aura. That is why people yearn for Paris, often without knowing that it is precisely this energy that they are looking for. We were always up to date and always felt that we were at the heart of everything, even when we did nothing but sit around in the cafés.”

It is possible to cross this city, which history and culture have given so much diversity and which owes its name to the Gallic tribe of the “Parisii”, on foot—from north to south or from east to west—in little more than two hours. But the most enchanting gateway to Paris is and remains the Seine river, which is spanned by thirty-seven bridges. Because the city is the “daughter of the Seine and of the king”, it first spread over the small islands and then along the banks of the big river that was such an ideal site for trade and commerce, and it adopted the proud and spirited motto “Fluctuat nec mergitur”—it is tossed by the waves, but does not sink.

Strolling along the Seine, or coming upon it once again, one has wonderful views of the city. From the top of a rise, the Palais de Chaillot, which embraces the fountains of the Jardins du Trocadéro, dominates the vista from the bridge named Pont d'léna. Behind the bridge, the Eiffel Tower rears above the green fields of the Champs de Mars, and the Dôme des Invalides is just a stone's throw away.

But sometimes one can leave this beautiful and classical route and open an gate that leads into a pristine park; or perhaps discover a small wineshop that serves cheese from the countryside; or find the entrance to one of the city's 150 museums—or the way to the quarter where antiquities are sold. And there, just as with the Parisian haute-couture labels, one is faced with the question of whether to merely admire so much creativity or to plunge oneself into financial ruin in order to possess it.

“This is not a city, this is a world of its own,” was an admiring aphorism during the Renaissance. Perhaps Paris has ever since been a city that incessantly brings new worlds to life.

Soraya Elyes Ferchichi

Paris, riesengroß und doch intim, ist Mythos und Stadt zugleich. Es zählt wie Rom, Jerusalem oder New York zu den Städten, die eine einzigartige, sich vollkommen von dem übrigen Land unterscheidende Identität entwickeln. Das hat wohl mit einer Lebenskunst zu tun, die zuallererst den Blick auf sich zieht: Das kreative und vielschichtige, verborgene und widersinnige Paris setzt die, die sich dort bewegen – gehetzte Bewohner der Stadt oder verzauberte Spaziergänger – unmittelbar in Szene. Manchmal sind es dieselben, nur zu einem anderen Zeitpunkt des Tages oder der Nacht, denn alles lädt hier zum Flanieren ein.

„Paris, das sind unschöpferische Orte und gesegnete Orte zugleich“, vertraute mir der Schriftsteller Lawrence Durrell an. „Die Stadt hat ein belebendes, faszinierendes und magnetisierendes Fluidum. Und deshalb sind die Menschen süchtig nach Paris, häufig ohne sich dessen bewusst zu sein, dass es gerade diese Energie ist, nach der sie suchen. Wir waren immer auf dem Laufenden, fühlten uns immer im Zentrum des Geschehens, selbst im Nichtstun, beim Herumsitzen auf den Caféterrassen.“

Diese aufgrund ihrer Geschichte und Kultur so vielseitige Stadt, die dem gallischen Stamm der „Parisii“ ihren Namen verdankt, kann man zu Fuß in etwas mehr als zwei Stunden von Nord nach Süd oder West nach Ost durchqueren. Aber der schönste Zugang zu Paris ist und bleibt die Seine, die 37 Brücken überspannen. Weil sie „Tochter der Seine und des Königs“ ist, hat sich die Stadt zunächst auf ihren kleinen Inseln, dann entlang dem für Tausch und Handel so günstig gelegenen, großen Fluss ausgebreitet, unter dem stolzen und munteren Motto „Fluctuat nec mergitur“: Er treibt dahin, ohne über die Ufer zu treten.

An der Seine entlangstreifend oder ihr wieder begegnend, all die großartigen Perspektiven der Stadt ... Von seinem Hügel grüßt das Palais de Chaillot, das die Springbrunnen der Jardins du Trocadéro umarmt, bis zur Pont d'Iéna. Hinter ihr erhebt sich der Eiffelturm aus seinem grünenden Schmuckkästchen, dem Champs de Mars, und ganz in der Nähe liegt der Invalidendom.

Aber manchmal kann man diese schöne, klassische Route verlassen, ein Hoftor aufstoßen, das sich zu einem urwüchsigen Park öffnet, vielleicht eine kleine Weinstube entdecken, die Bauernkäse anbietet, den Eingang eines der 150 Pariser Museen finden, oder aber auch den zum Antiquitätenviertel, wo man dann – wie bei einem der Pariser Haute-Couture-Labels – die Entscheidung treffen kann, so viel Kreativität nur zu bewundern oder sich dafür zu ruinieren.

„Dies ist keine Stadt, dies ist eine Welt“, entzückte man sich zu Zeiten der Renaissance. Vielleicht ist Paris seither eine Stadt, die unaufhörlich neuen Welten aufleben lässt.

Soraya Elyes Ferchichi

Paris, enorme y sin embargo, íntima. Mito y ciudad simultáneamente. Junto a Roma, Jerusalén o Nueva York, es una de esas ciudades que desarrollan una identidad única, perfecta y diferente al resto del país en que se encuentran. Esto guarda relación con un cierto arte de vivir, que en primera instancia atrae la atención. Paris, creativo y complejo, oculto y contradictorio, pone a todos sus apurados habitantes y sus ensoñados paseantes inmediatamente en escena. Algunas veces son las mismas personas, sólo en otro momento del día o de la noche, pues aquí todo invita a pasear.

"Paris tiene lugares benditos y abandonados al mismo tiempo…", me confesó el escritor Lawrence Durrell. "La ciudad posee un fluido tonificador, fascinante y magnético. Y por esta razón los seres humanos son adictos a Paris. En reiteradas ocasiones ni son conscientes que es esa la energía que están buscando. Siempre estábamos enterados de lo que ocurría, siempre nos sentíamos en el centro de los acontecimientos, aún sin hacer nada y sentados en las terrazas de las cafeterías."

Esta ciudad es polifacética debido a su cultura e historia, le debe su nombre a la etnia gálica "Parisi" y puede ser atravesada a pie en alrededor de dos horas de norte a sur y de este a oeste. Pero la más bella entrada a Paris fue y será el Sena, el río cruzado por 37 puentes. Dado que Paris es la "hija del Rey y el Sena", la ciudad se ha expandido en primer lugar hacia sus pequeñas islas y luego a lo largo del gran río, ideal para el intercambio y el comercio. Su lema orgulloso y vivo es "fluctuat nec mergitur": fluye sin salirse de su caudal.

A lo largo o cruzando el Sena se encuentran todas las maravillosas perspectivas de la ciudad… desde la colina saluda el Palacio de Chaillot, quien abraza las fuentes del Jardín de Trocadéro hasta Pont d´Iéna. Allí detrás se alza la Torre Eiffel en su verde caja de joyas, el Campo de Marte, y allí nomás queda la Catedral de Inválidos.

Pero algunas veces se puede abandonar esa ruta bella y clásica, abrir un portón que se abre a un parque abandonado, tal vez descubrir una pequeña bodega que ofrezca un queso de campo, encontrar la entrada de uno de los 150 museos o bien del barrio de los anticuarios, en donde uno, como en una de las marcas de alta costura parisina, puede tomar la decisión entre admirar tanta creatividad o bien arruinarse.

"No es una ciudad, es un mundo", se decía durante el Renacimiento. Tal vez, Paris sea desde entonces una ciudad que recrea mundos incesantemente.

Soraya Elyes Ferchichi

Parigi, sconfinata eppure raccolta, è mito e città insieme. È da annoverare tra quelle città come Roma, Gerusalemme o New York che sviluppano una propria, straordinaria personalità completamente differente da quella del resto del paese. Ha certo a che vedere con quel "savoir vivre" così ammirato : la creativa e dalle mille sfaccettature, nascosta e assurda Parigi pone immediatamente in primo piano tutti coloro che la attraversano, siano gli abitanti frenetici o i passanti incantati.

"Parigi è fatta di luoghi privi di ispirazione e di luoghi fecondi insieme", mi confidò lo scrittore Lawrence Durrell una volta. "Questa città emana un fluido corroborante, che affascina e avvince. E perciò si è attratti da Parigi, per lo più senza accorgersi che è proprio questa energia che si cerca. Si era sempre al corrente, ci si sentiva sempre al centro degli avvenimenti, perfino stando seduti sulle terrazze dei caffè, a non far nulla".

Questa città, che grazie alla sua storia e cultura è così multiforme e che deve il suo nome alla stirpe gallica dei Parisii, si attraversa a piedi in poco più di due ore, da nord a sud o da ovest ad est. Ma la più affascinante via d'accesso a Parigi è e rimane la Senna, attraversata da ben trentasette ponti. La città, "figlia della Senna e del re", si è estesa dapprima sulle piccole isole e poi lungo le sponde di quel fiume imponente, situato in una posizione favorevole per lo scambio e il commercio, secondo il detto orgoglioso e audace "fluctuat nec mergitur", scorre e si gonfia ma non straripa.

Passeggiando lungo la Senna o costeggiandola di tanto in tanto, ecco tutte le più grandiose vedute della città... Dalla sua collina arride il Palais de Chaillot, che abbraccia i getti d'acqua dei Jardins du Trocadéro, fino al Pont d'léna. Dietro di questo la Tour Eiffel si erge dal suo scrigno verdeggiante, lo Champs de Mars e poco più lontano si trova il Dôm des Invalides.

Talvolta, però, si può svicolare da questo classico e affascinante itinerario per imbattersi in un cancello che si apre su un parco selvatico, per scoprire forse una piccola osteria dove si offre del formaggio locale, o l'ingresso di uno dei centocinquanta musei parigini, o anche quello al quartiere degli antiquari, dove si può decidere, come in uno degli atelier d'alta moda parigini, di ammirare soltanto così tanta creatività o di andare in rovina.

"Non è una città, è tutto un mondo", dicevano ai tempi del Rinascimento. Da allora Parigi è forse diventa una città che dà incessantemente la vita a nuovi mondi.

Soraya Elyes Ferchichi

LIGNE N°1
RER
GARE DE LYON
LIGNE
RER
Le Train Bleu
Restaurant
Fruits de Mer

TAXI
PARISIEN

CHOREGRAPHIE
ACADEMIE NATIONALE DE MUSIQUE
POESIE LYRIQUE

PLAZA-ATHENEE

Dior

CHANEL

CAFE DE FLORE
LIPP

Café de Flore
CAFE DE FLORE
BOULEVARD SAINT GERMAIN

Les Deux Magots
Les Deux Magots

LE MOULIN DE LA VIERGE
Maison Mère Fondée en 1906
LE MOULIN DE LA VIERGE
PAIN SUR LEVAIN
FOUR A BOIS
FARINE DE MEULE
Spécialité de Pain Français
CROISSANTS
BRIOCHES
CHOCOLATINES
PAIN D'EPICES
MIEL
Blé Naturel

BOUCHERIE
BRANLY
ouvert

DIRON MONTPARNASSE
SORTIE
RUE DE VILLERSEXEL
12 49
PORTE DE
LA CHAPELLE
DANGER
116

BOULANGERIE
Fabrication

ECOLE SPECIALE DE

26 LZT 75

LIGNE
N°4
SAINT-MICHEL
LIGNE
N°4
METRO

Brasserie
MARS
AMERICAN

alma
alma

12F
GRAVURE
15F
18 CARTES
12F
35

1 = 10 Frs
3 = 25 Frs
MEUSE
PASTIS OLIVE
BIÈRES DE CHARTRES
BOURJOIS
CHAT NOIR
MOULIN ROUGE
BAL
LA GOULUE
AMBASSADEURS
aristide BRUANT
CHATS
Jardin d'Acclimatation
LE FROU-FROU
NICE
AÉROPOSTALE
Américaine
portative
CHAMPFLEURY · LES CHATS
SALLE WAGRAM
Jardin de Paris
CASINO DE PARIS
PARIS EN JOIE
PARIS-LONDRES

REPUBLIQUE
FRANCAISE

A VENDRE
4 Pièces
44 64 81 13
Le Parmentier

METROPOLITAIN
LE POINT
LE CHECK-UP
DE LA TERRE
HAVANA
COIFFURE

CITRONS
POIVRONS

Kronenbourg
Kronenbourg
RUE
SAINT SABIN
PARIS
LE PARIS
Kronenbourg Kronenbourg
ESTAURANT DE PARIS

19 JUILLET - 9 AOÛT
PARIS
QUARTIER
D'ÉTÉ
MAIRIE DE PARIS

92
BOULANGERIE PATISSERIE
GLACES
PAINS SPECIAUX
VIENNOISERIE

METRO
Patrick
BRUEL
FABRICE

NATIONALE
Louis XVI
un séjour
en
de la

CHANGE
RESTAURANT

AU BAROUDEUR
CAFE
ERES
RUE LA VIEUVILLE
OUVERT
Jour & Nuit
RICARD

BAR CHEZ
CREPES

MOULIN ROUGE
LA LOCO
FORMIDABLE
FORMIDABLE
FORMIDABLE
FORMIDABLE
LES DORISS GIRLS

JAMBONS
d'Origine
TRUFFES FRAICHES
&
Conservées
PIÈCES TRUFFÉES
sur
Commande
TERRINES
DE
Foies Gras
COMESTIBLES
DE
CHOIX
SAUCISSONS
DE
LYON & d'ARLES
FOIE GRAS
MAISON

JULIEN

NATIONAL

GALERIES LAFAYETTE

ESTÉE LAUDER
INTUITION

SIXTY
SIXTY

HERVE LEGER
HERVE
LEGER
PARIS

D·O·M·SVB·INVOC·S·M·MAGDALENAE

PAVILLON

ALERIE VERO-DODAT.
GALERIE VERO DODAT
Café de l'Epoque
STELLA ARTOIS
Café de l'Epoque
STELLA ARTOIS
RUE DU BOULOI

PASSAGE JOUFFROY
12
10
HOTEL RONCERAY
HOTEL RONCERAY
VISI EZ LES GALERIES
VISITEN LAS GALERIAS
VISIT THE GA
RONCERAY OPERA
BAR 'Le Rossini'
LA BOUTIQUE DES TUNIQUES

CAFÉ DU MÉTRO
depuis 1920
CAFÉ DU MÉTRO
depuis 1920
Le Monde
Les morts de Jénine pèsent sur la mission Colin Powell
Elysée 2002, la campagne
Venezuela : coup d'État contre Chavez
CAFÉ DU MÉTRO
depuis 1920

ATALYS

VINA
VINA

Table des matières Directory Verzeichnis Directorio Indice delle materie

62 Centre Georges-Pompidou (4e Arr.)

63 Centre Georges-Pompidou, Fontaine de Niki de Saint Phalle (4e Arr.)

64 Le Marais, Place des Vosges (4e Arr.)

65 Place de la République (3e Arr.)

66/67 Av. de la République (11e Arr.)

68 Quartier de la Bastille, Marché (11e Arr.)

Quartier de la Bastille, Marché (11e Arr.)

69 Quartier de la Bastille, Bistro « Le Paris » (11e Arr.)

70 Canal Saint-Martin (10e Arr.)

71 Canal Saint-Martin (10e Arr.)

72 Av. de la République, Boulagerie (11e Arr.)

73 Av. du Président-Wilson (16e Arr.)

Station du métro « Nationale » (13e Arr.)

74/75 Sacré-Cœur (18e Arr.)

76 Sacré-Cœur (18e Arr.)

77 Rue Foyatier (18e Arr.)

78 Rue la Vieuville, « Café au Baroudeur » (18e Arr.)

79 Place du Tertre (18e Arr.)

Place du Tertre (18e Arr.)

80 Sacré-Cœur (18e Arr.)

81 Bd. de Clichy, Moulin Rouge (18e Arr.)

82 Montmartre (18e Arr.)

83 Rue du Faubourg-Saint-Denis, Brasserie « Julien » (10e Arr.)

84 Rue du Faubourg-Saint-Denis, Brasserie « Julien » (10e Arr.)

85 Rue du Faubourg-Saint-Denis, Brasserie « Julien » (10e Arr.)

86 Bd. Haussmann, Galeries Lafayette (9e Arr.)

87 Bd. Haussmann, Galeries Lafayette (9e Arr.)

88/89 Saint-Germain-des-Prés, Bd. Saint-Germain (6e Arr.)

90 Rue du Faubourg-Saint-Honoré, Hervé Leger (8e Arr.)

91 La Madeleine (8e Arr.)

92 Palais du Louvre (1er Arr.)

Le Musée du Louvre, Cour Napoléon (1er Arr.)

93 Palais du Louvre (1er Arr.)

94 Quai du Louvre, Ile de la Cité et Pont Neuf (1er Arr.)

95 Rue Jean-Jaques-Rousseau, Galerie Vero-Dodat et « Café de l'Epoque » (1er Arr.)

96 Bd. Montmartre, Passage Jouffroy (9e Arr.)

97 Rue Vivienne, Galerie Vivienne (2e Arr.)

98/99 Palais du Louvre et Jardin des Tuileries (1er Arr.)

100 Jardin des Tuileries (1er Arr.)

101 Quai de la Mégisserie (1er Arr.)

102 Place de la Concorde (8e Arr.)

103 Saint-Germain-des-Prés, « Café du Métro » (6e Arr.)

104/105 Av. des Champs-Elysées et Palais du Louvre (8e Arr.)

106 Place Charles de Gaulle, Arc de Triomphe (8e Arr.)

107 Av. des Champs-Elysées et Palais du Louvre (8e Arr.)

108 Le Bois de Boulogne (16e Arr.)

109 La Défense, La Grande Arche

110 La Défense

111 La Défense

112/113 Le Métro, Bd. Vincent-Auriol (13e Arr.)

114 Seine, Pont de Bir Hakeim (15e Arr.)

115 Quai de Grenelle et Tour Eiffel (15e Arr.)

116/117 Musée d'Orsay (7e Arr.)

Front cover: Quartier de la Bastille, Bistro « Le Paris »
Back cover: Tour Eiffel et Hôtel des Invalides

Heiko Lanio Foto-Design
professional commercial & fine art photography
Nordwall 97, 47798 Krefeld
Germany
Phone/Fax: 00 49-(0) 21 51-78 62 06
www.lanio-foto-design.de
e-mail: info@lanio-foto-design.de

Photographs by Heiko Lanio, Krefeld
Design by Robert Kuhlendahl, teNeues Verlag
Introduction by Soraya Elyes Ferchichi, Paris
Translation by AMS · Hermann Scharnagl
Horst M. Langer (English)
Bettina Scharnagl (German)
Caterina Polito (Italian)
Eduardo C. Galimany (Spanish)
Editorial coordination by Sabine Würfel, teNeues Verlag
Color separation by O/R/T/, Krefeld, Germany

Die Deutsche Bibliothek – CIP-Einheitsaufnahme
Ein Titeldatensatz für diese Publikation ist bei der Deutschen Bibliothek erhältlich.

ISBN 3-8238-4519-5

Printed in Italy

Published by teNeues Publishing Group

teNeues Book Division
Neuer Zollhof 1
40221 Düsseldorf
Germany
Phone: 00 49-(0) 2 11-99 45 97-0
Fax: 00 49-(0) 2 11-99 45 97-40
e-mail: books@teneues.de
Press department: arehn@teneues.de
Phone: 00 49-(0) 21 52-916-202

teNeues Publishing Company
16 West 22nd Street
New York, N.Y. 10010
USA
Phone: 001-212-627-9090
Fax: 001-212-627-9511

teNeues Publishing UK Ltd.
Aldwych House
71/91 Aldwych
London WC2B 4HN
Great Britain
Phone: 0044-1892-837-171
Fax: 0044-1892-837-272

teNeues France S.A.R.L.
140, rue de la Croix Nivert
75015 Paris
France
Phone: 00 33-1-55 76 62 05
Fax: 00 33-1-55 76 64 19

www.teneues.com

teNeues Publishing Group
Kempen
Düsseldorf
London
New York
Paris

teNeues